D1523476

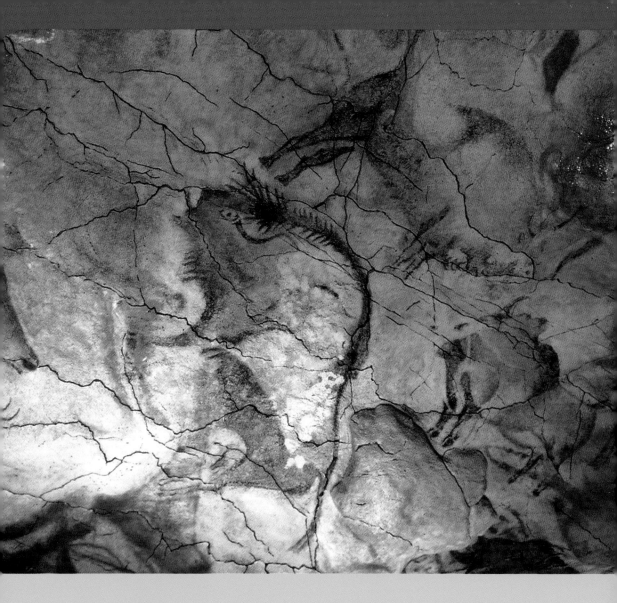

12 THINGS TO KNOW ABOUT
THE PALEOLITHIC ERA

by Meg Marquardt

STORY LIBRARY
MORE TO EXPLORE

www.12StoryLibrary.com

12-Story Library is an imprint of Bookstaves.

Photographs ©: Yvon Fruneau/CC3.0, cover, 1; Esteban De Armas/Shutterstock.com, 4; WolfmanSF/CC3.0, 5; Uncle Leo/Shutterstock.com, 5; Peter Maas/CC3.0, 6; Lillyundfreya/CC3.0, 7; Altaileopard/PD, 8; National Park Service, 9; Denis Bringard/Alamy, 10; Gary Todd/PD, 12; Vincent Mourre/CC3.0, 13; Gary Todd/PD, 14; Johnathan21/Shutterstock.com, 15; Ozja/Shutterstock.com, 16; Daniel Eskridge/Shutterstock.com, 16; Nicolas Primola/Shutterstock.com, 17; Craig Foster, 18; Daniel Maurer/Associated Press, 19; Rudolf Cronau/PD, 20; Wellcome Images/CC4.0, 21; José-Manuel Benito Álvarez/PD, 22; Morphart Creation/Shutterstock.com, 24; Morphart Creation/Shutterstock.com, 25; Chronicle/Alamy, 26; Heinrich Harder/PD, 27; Travel Update/YouTube, 29

ISBN
9781632357717 (hardcover)
9781632358806 (paperback)
9781645820529 (ebook)

Library of Congress Control Number: 2019938628

Printed in the United States of America
July 2019

About the Cover
Paleolithic cave art in northern Spain.

Access free, up-to-date content on this topic plus a full digital version of this book. Scan the QR code on page 31 or use your school's login at 12StoryLibrary.com.

Table of Contents

Early Humans Lived with Giant Sloths, Not Dinosaurs 4

Anatomically Modern Humans Came on the Scene 6

Humans Began in Africa 8

Early Humans Banded Together 10

Early Humans Made Tools to Solve Life's Problems 12

Eating Paleo Was Different Back Then 14

Animals Were More than Just Food 16

Early Humans Created Art and Clothes 18

Paleolithic Women Played Many Roles 20

Early Humans Buried Their Dead 22

The Paleolithic Era Had Climate Change Challenge 24

Early Humans Set Out to Sea and New Lands 26

Timeline of the Paleolithic Era 28

Glossary 30

Read More 31

Index 32

About the Author 32

Early Humans Lived with Giant Sloths, Not Dinosaurs

Movies sometimes paint a fantastic scene. People and dinosaurs roam the earth together. This is a cool image. However, it's totally imaginary. Humans and dinosaurs didn't live at the same time.

The big dinosaurs died out 65 million years ago. Human-like creatures didn't show up until 6 million years ago. By the time humans hit the scene, dinosaurs were long gone. No human ever saw a living Brontosaurus munching on plants. No one ever got chased by a T-Rex.

The world of ancient human-like beings was still strange and wild. Large mammals lived on all continents. There were giant sloths, armadillos, and porcupines. One of the best-known ancient mammals is the mammoth. Mammoths were like elephants. But they were at least twice as big as a modern elephant.

Six million years ago, some apes started to walk on two legs. This

Giant sloths weighed up to 4 tons (3.6 metric tons) and measured up to 20 feet (6 meters) tall.

4–7 million

Number of years ago when humans split from apes

- Humans share a common ancestor with today's apes, such as gorillas and chimpanzees.
- Scientists use genetics to figure out where and when the split happened.
- They look at skeletons to learn how the species walked, ate, and behaved.

is called bipedalism. It's one thing anthropologists think sets human-like creatures apart from other apes. Anthropologists know these early creatures were bipedal because of their skeletons. Clues in the skeletons make anthropologists think these beings held their head upright.

These early human-like creatures evolved over millions of years. Then, 300,000 years ago, a major change happened. Real humans were about to arrive.

2

Anatomically Modern Humans Came on the Scene

Modern-day humans have the scientific name *Homo sapiens*. It means "wise man." But modern humans weren't the first member of the *Homo* genus. There were ancient humans in Paleolithic times. They were the first to have human anatomy.

Anatomy is the study of body shape. Anthropologists studying skeletons look for anatomical clues. They can look at the shape of a bone. They can see if bones are missing.

206
Bones in the human body

- Just the hands and feet are made up of 106 bones.
- Babies have 300 bones at birth.
- Eventually, some bones fuse together.

These clues help them understand if a skeleton is human.

The fossil remains of "Java man," discoverd in Indonesia in 1891, are considered to be the oldest of the *Homo* genus.

The first anatomical clue is the leg bone. Thigh bones connect to hip bones. If a creature

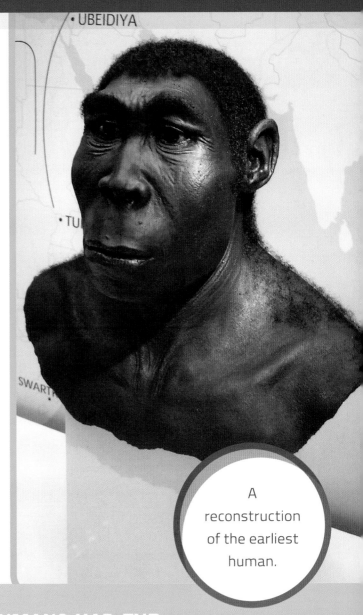

walks on all four limbs, the bone connects in a certain way. But if a creature walks on two legs, it connects in a different way. That is because a bipedal walker needs stronger support from their legs.

Members of the *Homo* genus also had bigger skulls. Bigger skulls mean bigger brains. Bigger brains gave early humans important advantages. A larger brain can have more complex thoughts. Today, human brains are three times as big as the brains of those early humans.

A reconstruction of the earliest human.

WHEN HUMANS HAD FUR

Humans are the only mammals without body hair or fur all over. But early humans probably were covered in fur. Some researchers think humans lost their fur to cut down on parasites. Ticks and other parasites love fur. Other researchers think humans lost their fur to keep their body temperature down. As early humans wandered over dry desert and grasslands, they needed less insulation. The less fur they had, the cooler they could be.

3

Humans Began in Africa

Humans started out in Africa about 200,000 years ago. They stayed mostly in Africa for more than 100,000 years. Then they began to travel.

Ancient humans might have left Africa because of droughts. They might have left because they were developing new tools and survival techniques. They were becoming smart enough to leave home and explore unknown places. Researchers aren't quite sure why these people left Africa. They think

these first travelers eventually populated the whole world.

From Africa, early humans headed to Arabia. Then they spread to India. Eventually, they made it to Europe. Travel was slow. Climates were icy. The further north they tried to go, the more wintery the weather became. Early humans didn't arrive in Europe until 40,000 years ago.

They traveled all over Europe and into Asia. The earth was still much colder than it is today. Sea levels were lower. They fell so low that a

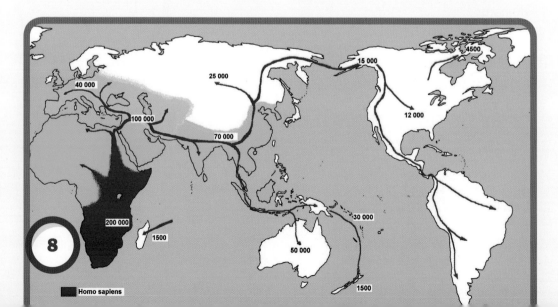

45000

15 000

25 000

40 000

12 000

100 000

70 000

30 000

200 000

1500

50 000

8

Homo sapiens

1500

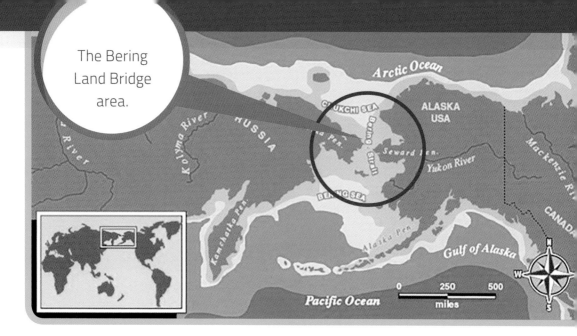

The Bering Land Bridge area.

land bridge connected Asia and North America. Researchers think Paleolithic people crossed over this land bridge.

300
How far in feet (91.4 m) water levels dropped to expose the Bering Land Bridge

- The land bridge was 1,000 miles (1,609.3 km) wide.
- The bridge meant that sea creatures like whales couldn't cross into southern waters.
- The bridge disappeared back under the sea 11,000 years ago.

OUR AFRICAN ANCESTORS

Researchers are now pretty certain that all humans originally came out of Africa. Early theories said that humans evolved from different pockets of people in different places. In 2003, small adult skeletons were discovered in Asia. Some researchers thought humans might have also evolved from these small people. But by looking at DNA, researchers have discovered that modern humans only came from Africa.

4

Early Humans Banded Together

Reconstruction of what a Paleolithic hut might have looked like.

As early humans left Africa, they faced new challenges. But they didn't face them alone. Paleolithic humans traveled in small bands. Food could be scarce, so the bands couldn't be too big. Researchers think there were about 25 people in these early groups. Members would be in charge of different tasks. Some might be hunters. Others might take care of children. Still others might gather food or build shelters.

Paleolithic people built huts out of straw and mud. They also built some structures made of wood or the bones of big animals. These structures might be split into different sections. Think of them as early studio apartments. There were no walls to block the bedroom from the kitchen. There was a place for sleeping, a place for eating, and a place for gathering.

That people grouped together suggests another important fact. It's likely these prehistoric people had some sort of language. It's hard to tell exactly when humans developed the ability to speak. Humans have a voice box in their throat. The voice box isn't made of bone. It doesn't survive in fossils. However, to have a complex society, people need to be able to talk about building, hunting, and their fellow band members. Anthropologists are pretty sure that by the Paleolithic era, people were talking to one another.

1
People per square mile (2.6 square kilometers)—the population density—in Paleolithic times

- Paleolithic populations grew slowly.
- Caring for children required a lot of work.
- Fertility rates were low.

THINK ABOUT IT

If your city only had 25 people in it, how different might it look? What jobs might disappear?

5

Early Humans Made Tools to Solve Life's Problems

Hammerstones helped break off pieces of other stones to make sharp tools and spears.

The Paleolithic era is also called the Old Stone Age. That's because early humans used stone tools. This might not seem like a big deal. But the use of stone tools gave humans an important advantage.

Tools help people solve problems. Some nuts can only be eaten if their shell is cracked open. A human might think to smash a rock against the nut to crack its

shell. In the process, the nut's meat gets messed up with the shell. That means the human can't eat as much of the nut's meat. If that human could invent a nutcracking tool, they would get more nut out of each crack.

One of the best tools in the Paleolithic tool kit was the hammerstone. Hammerstones were usually big, hand-sized rocks. They were made of very hard rock. They

3,600
Number of stone tools found on the Tibetan Plateau in 2018

- The tools were found by a Chinese research team.
- The team was exploring the oldest and highest known Paleolithic archaeological site.
- Thin air and cold temperatures make the Tibetan Plateau one of the harshest environments on earth.

HUMANS AREN'T THE ONLY TOOL USERS

Using tools isn't unique to humans. The earliest known stone tool dates back 3.3 million years. Archaeologists think our human ancestors were using tools. Biologists have also discovered that certain primates and even birds use tools. This is a sign of a bright mind. Humans might be the smartest creature, but they aren't alone.

were so hard they could break off pieces of other stones.

Paleolithic hunters would heat up a stone called silcrete in fire. Then they would hit the hot silcrete with hammerstones. The silcrete would break away in flakes. The flakes were rocks with very sharp edges. They could be used to make spears for hunting.

These silcrete points found in a cave in South Africa date to 73,000 years ago.

Eating Paleo Was Different Back Then

In 2012, an article was published in a scientific journal about nutrition. The article asked, "Are Diets from Paleolithic Times Relevant Today?" That might seem like a silly question. But a new diet fad was sweeping the world. It's called the Paleo Diet or the Caveman Diet. People who follow it claim that eating only what our ancient ancestors ate is the healthiest option. They eat a ton of meat, vegetables, and fruit. They don't eat any dairy products, most grains, or sugar.

Researchers think modern paleo eaters don't understand how Paleolithic people really ate. Ancient vegetables were much different from today's vegetables. Most were much smaller. For example, potatoes were about as big as shelled peanuts. Many other vegetables were covered in spikes, thorns, or bristles. Some were poisonous. In short, most Paleolithic people weren't chowing down on veggies.

Paleolithic people were skilled hunters.

Grinding seeds and grains made them easier to eat.

They were hunting for a lot of meat, though. Those hunters were skilled at killing large deer, cow-like creatures, and horses. They also were strong fishers.

30
Life expectancy in years of early Paleolithic people

- Researchers can learn from studying skeletons how old people were when they died.
- Looking at the amount of wear on someone's teeth gives them clues.
- Better tools and living in groups helped people live longer.

Ancient humans also ate grains. Researchers know that Paleolithic people ate seeds from grasses. In modern times, humans eat seeds from grasses like wheat. In Paleolithic times, these seeds would have been tougher to eat, even if they were cooked. Researchers have found evidence of stone grinders in China. These grinders were used by people 20,000 years ago. They would have ground up the grain seeds to make them more edible.

THINK ABOUT IT

Imagine that you live in Paleolithic times. What skills do you need to find food?

Animals Were More than Just Food

Woolly rhinos and woolly mammoths were hunted for their pelts.

Early humans hunted animals for food. But the animal world was weird and wild. Not every interaction with animals was about finding food. Paleolithic humans also used animals for clothing and companionship.

Some animals who roamed had woolly coats. They were covered in long, thick fur. That fur helped protect them from the harsh, cold climates many lived in. There were woolly mammoths and woolly rhinos.

Humans hunted animals for their warm, woolly pelts. Some researchers think early people also used pelts for rugs. Researchers found a site with ancient lion toe bones. There were marks on the bones that made the researchers think the bones had once been attached to a pelt. The bones were in

GIANT BUGS

Before dinosaurs and long before humans, there were giant bugs. They ruled the Paleozoic era 300 million years ago. There were dragonflies as large as hawks. Millipedes could be bigger than a human leg. Researchers think these bugs died out because oxygen levels lowered. With less oxygen, the bugs couldn't thrive.

Bugs were much bigger in the Paleozoic era.

a cave thought to be an important religious site. That led researchers to think that the Paleolithic people who lived there used the pelt in a religious ceremony.

There is also evidence that Paleolithic people were domesticating dogs. Researchers found the remains of a dog with two human remains. The dog appeared to have been sick. Researchers believe that the dog had been cared for by those humans.

12
Width in feet (3.7 m) of an Irish elk's antlers

- Irish elks roamed Europe.
- They could be up to 7 feet (2.1 m) tall.
- The species went extinct 11,000 years ago.

Early Humans Created Art and Clothes

One of the oldest known pieces of art is a stone. It was found in a cave in South Africa. This stone is covered in small red lines. The lines match a hatch pattern. A hatch pattern looks like a bunch of hashtags. Archaeologists think the pattern was drawn with a red crayon-type tool. It's over 70,300 years old.

Cave art from the Paleolithic era is impressive. Some of the most famous examples are at Chauvet-Pont-d'Arc in southern France. That location has two huge caves. On the walls are paintings of animals. Rhinos charge at each other. Herds of horses gallop along. There are owls, lions, and deer. Most of the drawings were made with charcoal and red clay.

Paleolithic people also made small statues. These statues were often of women. Scholars aren't sure why. Maybe Paleolithic people were just trying to make something beautiful. Maybe they were used in religious rituals. Maybe they were symbols of fertility.

Archaeologists have found some evidence of early clothing.

The stone art that was found in a cave in South Africa.

THE FIRST MUSIC

Art is a sign of culture and society. Art is a way to form an identity. Paleolithic people were taking time to create. They also made music. A 35,000-year-old bone flute was found in Germany. This flute was made from a bird bone. Researchers think the flute proves that music was an important part of life, even back then.

The bird bone flute is the oldest handcrafted musical instrument ever discovered.

Clothes don't fossilize well. They are made from plants and furs. Those materials break down. But there have been some discoveries of dyed fibers. These fibers were in pinks and blues. Archaeologists think they might have been used for clothing.

82,000
Age in years of the oldest known piece of art

- The oldest piece of art is a necklace.
- It is made of snail shells dyed red.
- The necklace was found in Morocco.

Paleolithic Women Played Many Roles

How did Paleolithic people divide up their work? For a long time, researchers believed that men hunted and women stayed home and took care of the children. This belief was colored by stereotypes and misinformation.

In the 1990s, researchers began to rethink the part Paleolithic women played. They took a new look at their data. They went back and reread accounts written by people who observed modern-day hunter-gatherer societies. They went out and made new observations.

The researchers found that Paleolithic women probably played a big role in society. Women helped with hunting. They set traps to catch small game. They dug up roots to eat. They also watched over children. They helped keep home camps safe

Researchers now think woman played a bigger role in the Paleolithic era.

ANCIENT ARTISTS

Researchers once thought that most Paleolithic statues were made by men. But new research suggests that women were making art, too. Some art historians think the statues were made by women modeling their own bodies. The statues look like a female's perspective of looking down at her own body. That's why hips and breasts are larger than normal.

A Paleolithic statue that researchers think was made by a woman.

and productive. Researchers now think that men and women did an equal amount of labor.

Researchers realized that most of their data had been about men. They hadn't really looked closely at women's roles. This created a bias. Women didn't look like they played a big role because no one had asked questions about them. By finding new ways to look at data, researchers were able to better understand the Paleolithic era.

41,000
Age in years of hand stencils found in Spain's El Castillo Cave

- Researchers compared some of the stencils.
- They looked at the lengths of certain fingers.
- They concluded that some of the stencils were made by women.

21

Early Humans Buried Their Dead

Imagine that you're an archaeologist. After carefully digging through layers of dirt, you find a grave site. There's a human skeleton inside. But that's not all. There is jewelry made of stone. There are household items like stone tools. The grave is a snapshot of Paleolithic life.

Graves are one reason researchers know so much about the Paleolithic era. Other early human-like people

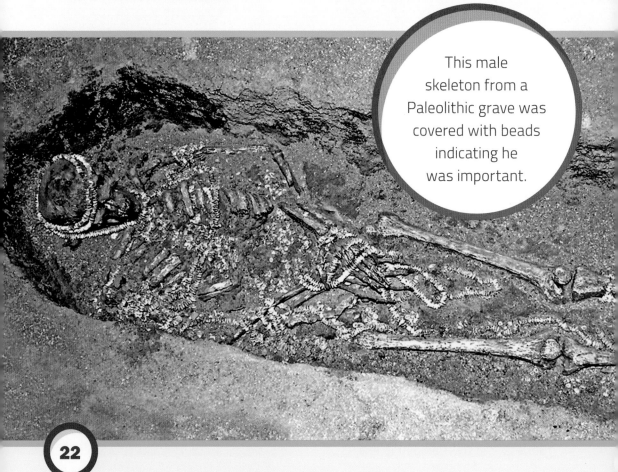

This male skeleton from a Paleolithic grave was covered with beads indicating he was important.

didn't often bury their dead. Over time, unburied remains are washed away, broken up, or carried off by animals. But a grave keeps everything together.

Graves tell us a lot about early culture. Some grave sites are very elaborate. This suggests that early humans took part in rituals. Different people were buried in different ways. For example, a body in Russia was found covered in thousands of beads. At the same site, other bodies were barely buried and had no beads. Researchers think the man covered with beads must have been important to the group. The others were less important. Burial rituals changed based on who was being buried.

Just because Paleolithic people had burial rituals doesn't mean they practiced religion. Because there was no writing in Paleolithic times, it's close to impossible to know what

300,000
Age in years of the oldest known human fossils

- The fossils were found in Morocco.
- These fossils changed how researchers thought people migrated.
- *Homo sapiens* lived in almost all of Africa by 300,000 years ago.

people believed in. But burial rituals might show some kind of religious belief. Some gravesites look like they were protected. Paleolithic people also took great care to bury the skull, more than other parts of the body. So maybe they were religious. But it's impossible to say for certain.

11

The Paleolithic Era Had Climate Change Challenges

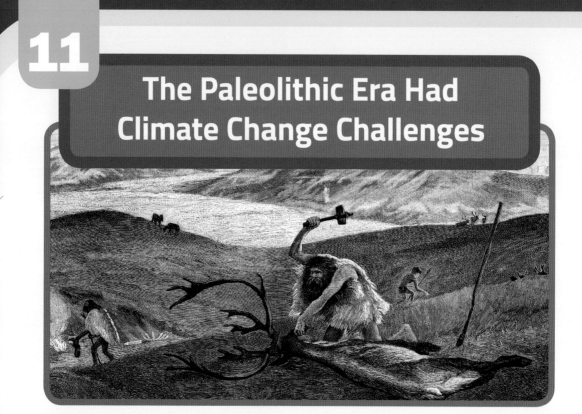

The earth's climate changed a lot during the Old Stone Age. One of the biggest challenges Paleolithic people faced were mini-ice ages. During a true ice age, the world would be very cold and dry. A lot of water would be trapped in ice. A true ice age could last millions of years. Life during this time would have been hard.

Mini-ice ages aren't quite so drastic. They don't last as long and aren't as cold. But they still create harsh conditions. Some areas of the planet would have been unlivable. Plants and animals would

have died. Humans would have needed to adapt.

Climate change may have caused humans to evolve. Researchers think bigger brains might have developed as a result of climate challenges. Another neat possibility is that climate changes caused humans to start walking upright. Africa used to be more covered in trees. During a warming period, it became more like a grassland. Instead of climbing trees, pre-human primates would have had to walk.

One thing is certain: Humans needed the ability to deal with changing climates. As the world warmed, some types of food would disappear. Early humans needed to be able to eat and digest different types of food. Human teeth changed as warming periods brought more vegetation to eat. Researchers can't tie climate change directly to these changes. But they think climate had an effect.

Climate also affected animals. During an icy period, big elephant-like mastodons had to leave their arctic homes. They needed more food to graze on. Glaciers were starting to cover their food source. Moving south meant they ran into humans. Humans started to hunt them. Between humans and climate change, mastodons went extinct.

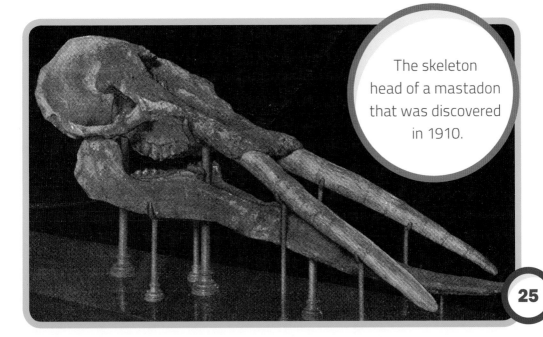

The skeleton head of a mastadon that was discovered in 1910.

Early Humans Set Out to Sea and New Lands

During prehistoric times, the world went through cycles of cooling and warming. In cold times, a lot of water was trapped in ice. The seas were lower, and some places were connected by land bridges. For example, Britain was once linked to mainland Europe. There were still some places that could only be reached by water. Because of this, researchers know that pre-humans built boats. The first boat building may have happened as early as 800,000 years ago.

Paleolithic people built more sophisticated boats. They were likely specialized canoes and rafts. These boats could be easily tied together with strong vines. They would have been made from wood or reeds. They probably would have been pushed by poles and paddles. They may have had simple sails. They might not have gotten very far. But

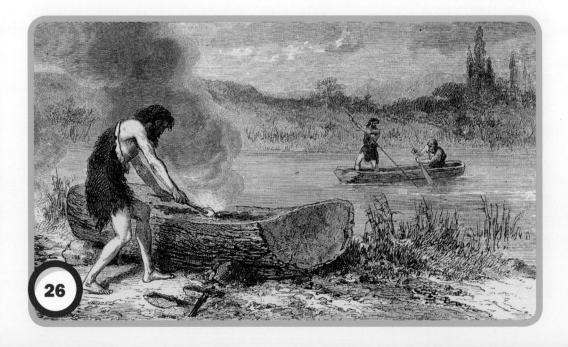

2,000

Number of stone tools found on the island of Crete

- Crete is an island that can only be reached by traveling across the Mediterranean Sea.
- The tools were 130,000 years old.
- Paleolithic people must have sailed to the island.

THINK ABOUT IT

Prehistoric people built their own boats to cross water. What would you use to build a boat to travel to a new land?

Giant armadillos were common in the Americas at the time Paleolithic people arrived.

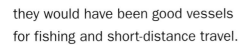

they would have been good vessels for fishing and short-distance travel.

Paleolithic people came to the Americas by a land bridge. They found a host of new and strange animals. There were huge armadillos and sloths. There were also giant wolves called dire wolves, and big saber-toothed cats.

Timeline of the Paleolithic Era

The Paleolithic Era—the Old Stone Age—lasted from 2.6 million years ago to about 12,000 years ago. That is a long stretch of time. Scientists have split it into three chunks. They call them the Lower, Middle, and Upper Paleolithic.

2.6 million to 250,000 years ago: Lower Paleolithic

2.6 million years ago:
Early humans are making and using stone tools. Researchers have found stone tools that are even older.

400,000 to 300,000 years ago:
Humans start creating fire for heat and cooking.

315,0000 years ago:
Researchers have found *Homo sapiens* remains that date to this time. Modern humans are *Homo sapiens*. These remains were a surprise. They are 100,000 years older than previous remains.

250,000 to around 50,000 years ago: Middle Paleolithic

200,000 years ago:
Humans are making more sophisticated stone tools. Their homes are more complex. Researchers think this points to more complex societies.

170,000 years ago:
Humans are wearing clothing.

82,000 years ago:
Earliest known example of jewelry. The necklace is a string of seashell beads.

50,000 to 12,000 years ago: Upper Paleolithic

50,000 years ago:
Humans are using tools made of bones and antlers. They are making bone needles.

20,000 years ago:
First evidence of pottery. It was found in a cave in China.

12,000 years ago:
Humans have arrived in America and Australia.

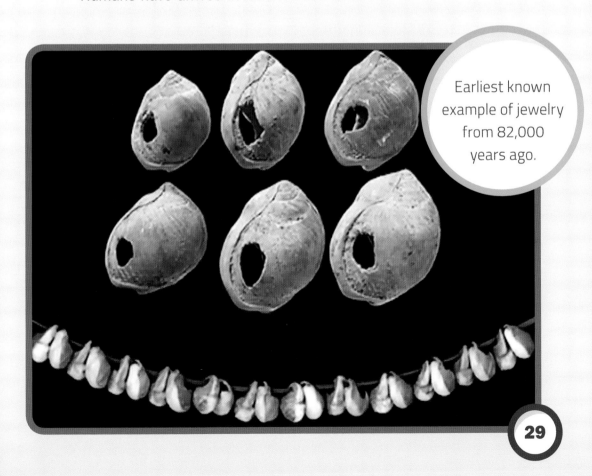

Earliest known example of jewelry from 82,000 years ago.

Glossary

adapt
Respond to outside forces, like changing temperatures.

anthropologist
Someone who studies ancient human culture.

archaeologist
Someone who studies ancient artifacts.

bias
Showing favor for one side of an argument.

fertility
The ability to have babies.

fibers
Threads made out of vegetables.

game
Animal meat.

genetics
The study of how certain features are passed from parents to their young.

genus
A group of plants and animals that are related.

mammal
Animals that have fur, produce milk, and give birth to live young

parasite
An animal or plant that lives on or inside another living creature and gets its food from it.

pelt
An animal's skin with the fur still on.

ritual
A special ceremony.

stereotype
An oversimplified idea of a person or group.

Read More

Felix, Rebecca. *Unearthing Early Human Remains*. Minneapolis, MN: ABDO Publishing, 2019.

Ganeri, Anita. *Writing History: Stone Age*. London, UK: Franklin Watts, 2019.

Mooney, Carla. *Evolution: How Life Adapts to a Changing Environment*. River Junction, VT: Nomad Press, 2017.

Visit 12StoryLibrary.com

Scan the code or use your school's login at **12StoryLibrary.com** for recent updates about this topic and a full digital version of this book. Enjoy free access to:

- Digital ebook
- Breaking news updates
- Live content feeds
- Videos, interactive maps, and graphics
- Additional web resources

Note to educators: Visit 12StoryLibrary.com/register to sign up for free premium website access. Enjoy live content plus a full digital version of every 12-Story Library book you own for every student at your school.

Index

anatomy, 6-7
ancestors, 5, 8-9, 13, 14
armadillos, 4, 27
apes, 5

Bering Land Bridge, 9
boats, 26-27

cave art, 18, 21
climate, 8, 16, 24-25
clothing, 16, 18-19, 28

evolution, 5, 9

food, 10, 14-15, 25
fossils, 6, 23

genetics, 5, 28
giant bugs, 17
graves, 22-23

Homo sapiens, 6
hunters, 13, 14-15, 20
huts, 10-11

ice ages 24-25

language, 11
life expectancy, 15

mastodons, 25
mammoth, 4, 16
music, 19

pelts, 16

roles of women, 20-21

sloths, 4
statues, 18, 21

tools, 12-13, 22, 27, 28-29
travel, 8, 10, 27

woolly rhinos, 16
woolly mammoths, 16

About the Author

Meg Marquardt started out as a scientist but likes writing about science even more. She enjoys researching physics, geology, and climate science. She lives in Madison, Wisconsin, with her two scientist cats, Lagrange and Doppler.